Pterodactyls.

7.99   6c/41

An African Elegy

AN AFRICAN ELEGY

Ben Okri

JONATHAN CAPE
LONDON

First published 1992
© Ben Okri 1992
Jonathan Cape, 20 Vauxhall Bridge Road, London sw1v 2sa

Ben Okri has asserted his right under
the Copyright, Designs and Patents Act, 1988
to be identified as the author of this work.

Poems in this collection have appeared in the
following publications: *Grandchildren of Albion,
PEN International, The Times,* the *Guardian,
Colours of a New Day, West Africa Magazine*

A CIP catalogue record for this book
is available from the British Library

ISBN 0–224–03006–x

Printed in Great Britain by
Mackays of Chatham PLC, Chatham, Kent

Contents

Lament of the Images

They took the masks
The sacrificial faces
The crafted wood which stretches
To the fires of natural gods
The shrines where the axe
Of lightning
Releases invisible forces
Of silver.

They took the painted bones
The stools of molten kings
The sacred bronze leopards
The images charged with blood
And they burned what
They could not
Understand.

They burned
All that frightened them
In the ferocious power
Of ancient dreams
And all that held
The secrets
Of terror
And all that battled
With dread
In the land
And all that helped
The crops
Sprout
All that spoke
To the gods
In their close
And terrifying

Distance
They burned them all
They burned them in heaps
They burned them in alien piety.

They took some images
And brought them across
The whitening seas
And stored them in
Basements
For the later study
Of the African's
Dark and impenetrable
Mind.
They called them
'Primitive objects'
And subjected them
To the milk
Of scientific
Scrutiny.

2

The Images died in spirit
And contorted
Their faces
In the Western
Darkness.

In their native lands
Other Images were made
For new seasons
A new god
For a new
Age.

And when the Images began
To speak
In forgotten tongues
Of death
The artists of the alien
Land
Twisted the pain
Of their speech
And created a new
Chemistry
Which, purified of ritual
Dread,
They called
Art.

3

The secret places
Of the African's
Dark and impenetrable
Mind
Touch the spirits
Of the deepest night.
The masks still live
Still speak
And only a few
Can hear them
Hear the terror of their
Chants
Which breed powers
Of ritual darkness
And light
In the centre
Of the mind's
Regeneration.

The makers of Images
Kept their secrets well
For since the departure
Of the masks
The land
Has almost
Forgotten
To chant its ancient songs
Ceased to reconnect
The land of spirits.

4

And the spirits
Hunger
For our touch
Our contact.
The spirits
In their
Loneliness
Have begun
To go insane
They possess
Our minds
They grip our dreams
They weigh down
The flights
Of our inventions.
And every now and again
We break out
In strange tongues.
Rashes
Of violence
Streak across
Our continent

And hang over our
Skies.

The makers of Images
Dwell with us still
We must listen
To their speech
Re-learn their
Songs
Recharge the psychic
Interspaces
Of our dying
Age
Or live dumb
And blind
Devoid of old
Song
Divorced from
The great dreams
Of the magic and fearful
Universe.

An Undeserved Sweetness

After the wind lifts the beggar
From his bed of trash
And blows him to the empty pubs
At the road's end
There exists only the silence
Of the world before dawn
And the solitude of trees.

Handel on the set mysteriously
Recalls to me the long
Hot nights of childhood spent
In malarial slums
In the midst of potent shrines
At the edge of great seas.
Dreams of the past sing
With voices of the future.

And now the world is assaulted
With a sweetness it doesn't deserve
Flowers sing with the voices of absent bees
The air swells with the vibrant
Solitude of trees who nightly
Whisper of re-invading the world.

But the night bends the trees
Into my dreams
And the stars fall with their fruits
Into my lonely world-burnt hands.

The Cross is Gone
For R.C.

It was a day of fairs
Yellow music on the wind, feathers
Of dead birds whirling beyond
The green trees.

We walked up into the Heath
Passed a man riding a baby's bicycle
And the paths confused us.
It had rained; the earth was soggy
Beneath the deceptive grass.
We strayed past trees that bore
The features of dying men.

All around us the trees were heaving.
Their comrades had fallen
The great spirits trapped in their monstrous
Trunks sang in the cold air
Songs of white mermaids
Corrupted beyond their time.
Their comrades had fallen:
They who had witnessed the sordidness
And the miracles of three hundred years
Felled in an instant of nightspace
By the karmic hurricanes
Of an unconfronted history.

Like old elephants, their trunks inscrutable,
Breathing lamentations on the unforgiving earth
Into which they will not be reborn,
The trees sang to us of a darkening age
With mysteries dying
And yellow spirits in the wind.

We passed their hulks

On the graveyard of the Heath
We said nothing about them
We talked about a single voice
From oppressed spaces
That could bring down thunder on corrupt lands
And about tyranny unleashing wounds on itself
That bleed through us, the innocent journeyers
Into forbidden zones of dying gods.

We passed them quickly
Noting the character and psychology
Of each surviving tree —
Then, from the valley, we looked up high
And saw three kites,
One red, another of blue,
The third of gold, invisibly attached
To a black cross,
Bold against the sky.

We climbed Parliament Hill
Our spirits heaving, our breaths
Quickening, the earth slipping beneath our feet.
The sky quivered with silent birds.
With our ascent we noticed a gathered crowd,
An old woman with a yellow scarf
A black man with a red beret on his bald head
Children playing with strings
A nun with frozen hands
An Irish priest wearing metal-framed glasses
An enormous bible under his arm
A wand in one hand, the string of the red
Kite in the other.

We approached them, holding

Fast to our invisible trail, breathing
Heavily the rarefied air:
And when we gained the hill top
The cross shivered
A strong wind, smelling of incense and radiation,
And disease and French perfume and hidden wars,
Blew over from the distant Thames.

We saw all the world laid out
Before us in the air
A city perceived in a moment's enchantment
Whose history, weighed down with guilt and machines,
Laughed all around us like ghosts
Who do not believe in the existence
Of men.

We saw the city and marvelled.
We dream the city better
Than it dreams itself.
The air and distance weave such burning
Miracles from the houses and church spires
The towers and glass offices of multinationals.
We dream the housing estates, built on marshes;
The woods, sad and defiant;
The disorder of buildings, the threaded streets,
Where madmen wander alone,
Where men dream of impossible women,
And women of non-existent men,
With each pursuing instant fulfillment
Love without responsibility
Miracles without pain
Transformation without humility
Joy without despair
Power without vulnerability

Fame without chaos
A new life without a new death
Difficult dreams, doomed to abortions
And sick births
Blind births, one-eyed births.
In the phantasm of the city
Glacial vision prevails
While voices from the marshes vainly cry out
That they are the victims and hostages
Of the history their parents accepted
In silence.

The world lay before us
And the wind stayed still.
We wandered round the Irish priest
Not daring to approach
How would we be received?
And then a bitter wind blew the kites
And one got stuck, blue on green, against
The branches of a fallen tree —
We wandered round the crowd
And gazed at the cross
Upon which was written, on that wintry day,
Summery with the blessedness of its naming —
For it was Easter Sunday —
The words, clear as glass:

> Christ has died
> Christ is risen
> Christ will come again –

And our spirits soared, mixing with the clouds
Of deep colour —
A child's cry of delight
Sent the golden kite upwards.

The priest's cassock lifted and was whipped
By the winds of four directions.
Voices became sweet on the air.
In the distance below, the three lakes
Shimmered — the wind carved its many names
On the face of the waters.

We went down and dwelled
In the solitude of swans.
We talked of painting, love, and adventures.
My friend's face was reddened by her red coat.
We heard the fair and followed the jangling music
Through the wet trails
And came upon cacophony.
We dwelled in the fair, listened to the conflicting
Noises, watched the faces of ticket sellers,
And the machines like windmills sending
The children into the air
Of artificial stimulation
And the gadgets and games and bumper cars
That once filled our adolescence with longing
But which left us hungry and empty now.

We left the fair followed by the smell
Of mass-cooked sausages, by dogs
Dragging hamburgers between their teeth —
We left the day behind us, with the view
From Parliament Hill
Forever bright in our vision.
We went back to our lives of ordinary miracles
With the joy of that day lost in us
Till three days later when she returned
From a long walk —
She didn't look sad, or disappointed:

But in that tone of voice we reserve
For events that should be underlined
Except we don't know why
Or how, or with what accentuation
To underline them
Make them speak
Make them significant —
And with a disturbed, imperceptible tossing
Of her head
A movement of her shoulders
A hand launching itself into the air
But holding back
She said, simply, without mystery:
               'The cross — that cross — is gone.'

April 1988

We Sing Absurdities

For Robert Fraser

We sing absurdities
On the face
Of anguish
And enact cameos
Within the eye's
Vision.

We sing of absurdities —
Arabesques of bodies
Entangled
In the dissolutions
And vapours
Of power:
Victims of seepages
And batterings from above.

We sing absurdities
When all else sinks in shallows.
Word–acids dissolve
Ordinary chaos:
Within the eye

A potent chemistry
Unmasks the faces
Beneath the terrors
And fills the silences
Of anguished journeys.
Dreams live serenely
In our singing
And our eyes.

We sing absurdities
When all else sinks in shallows.

Stammerings on Bedrock

Karma proceeds upwards
Through skies of aquamarine terrors;
The world loops under
Bringing the tyranny of rain
Upon the heads of priests
And upon the rest of us
The mania of a planet ruled
By fear.

Rain wisdom down upon the earth
Wash thunder upon us
And on this landscape smash
Our beginnings:
Smash the endings that they foresaw
Hold us in the palm of incandescent
Understanding
Bare us to those birds of madness
That peck at our false bindings
And reveal the pulp of flesh
Our cross of fire.
Explode to us our history
Save us from our resourceful
Damnation.

2

I have seen lies grow from
Seeds of twisted dreams
They shoot up in ordinary nights
They gorge themselves upon our hunger
We feed ourselves on their poisons.

I have seen destruction
Sown in the fields.
Birds murdered in innocent flight

Withhold the rain.
The priests raise songs.
The sky touches the bird's wings
With fingers of the rainbow.
Mythology reclaims the terrors;
The priests raise dust:
Rain answers with floods.

I have seen the fields
Light up to simple truths:
That dreams proliferate our graveyards.
Dictators officiate.
Our history has bred
Diseased raptors.
And our survivals have given
Rise to chimerical monsters.
The chalice of bad faith
Overflows.

3

We have risen warped at dawn
And seen masquerades weave their dreams
With our anger
At our lily-headed ancestors.
How they betrayed us:
How we betray ourselves.
And who can project an understanding
Of the small dangerous things
Stealing their shadows
Over the terrain?
Who can rouse the memories
Of dead animals
Rotting in the fields
And the drops of bad milk dripping

Into the mouths
Of ghost-ridden children?
Harmattan grips the lights.
The sound of thunder stirs recollections:
Cataclysms forefelt blow over our bodies.

Our fears at dawn distort
The sound beneath the streets
And betray a solemn transformation
From festivity
To the very home of the Iron mask.
Failures and misdirections
Flow from the forest fires
And the political funfairs.

Whispering treetrunks are silenced
In the burning of witches
Over fires choked
With the hair of the strangers
In our midst.
We tear apart the flesh
Of us, the strangers approaching
Who bring superstition
With every gesture.

Always there are intimations
Of war after rain.
And who can hear the snakes
Whisking under
Isolated huts?
Who can interpret the rabble
Of foxes?
Who can bear the weight
Of too much significance

Too many signs?
Who can see the destiny
Of our fevers
And give them shape?
Who will announce the deformation
Of our dreams?
Treetops weave cruciform in dry air.
Masquerades fall from ancestral heights.
Politicians deny our doom.

4

The rains drive in a new fever.
The feet thrashing in the sky
Will surely collapse into
The awful gravity of the rainmaker.
And we must walk over the graves
Of prophets
And listen to the agonies of those
Who accept.
We must watch the greenery
Of our laughter
And calculate the length of time
Between the rumbles of our stomachs
And the riots in the fields.
The birds descend keening.
We are with them.

The pressure of necessity
The strange violence of need
Quaking the marketplaces and the palaces
Will grace our anger with love.
The bellowings in the sky
Touch the fields
With fresh anguish:

Hold us all in the palm
Of incandescent understanding.

The anguish from the arteries
Of the streets
Is spreading our hunger
From here to a new highway.
The wonder of the birds
Falling in the midst
Of our cataclysm
Infests our bedrock
With heat.

Upon these times smash our lies.
Bare us to our naked highways.
Thundershine lights the fields:
We can reclaim our lives.

Little Girl

Little girl
In the green river
I watch you
Bathing away the last
Smiles of initiation
With ripples of the water's cruelty
Catching
The wondrous lights
From the sky.

Little girl
In the savage river
I marvel that you float
In silvery state
Amongst the riverweed
And fishes:
I marvel more
At seeing you smiling across
To the boatman
Whirling in the currents
Who drowned while sleeping
Who dreamed of the source
And of you.

I see the gashes on your face
The marks you can't explain
Or wonder at
For the river gives off no reflections;
The fever in your eyes
Calls me
From my watchpost
In this time of drought;
I descend
And find the waves

Are raging
A new fear, a terrible understanding.

The fishes have all gone
The weeds have gathered themselves away
I see you startled
At the stillness that comes
When the animals plunge
Into the river
To remain with you:
And I understand your terror.

Little girl
In the flowering river
You have found
An alcove in the whirlpool:
It seemed such a neutral place
For your last rites
Before the howls in the air
Discover your secrets.

And now that it is all over
And the animals bulk the shoreline
And the pillows of the riverbed
Whisper a great unease
And the river has reversed its current
And now that you can float
To all the cities
Under the darkening sky
There is one thing I have to tell you:

On my way back up
The watchpost had been destroyed
And a crumbling new tower erected.

There was a feast of madmen
And many tongues sang of abundant chaos
In the orgies
While there has been
So much water
From your eyes
In the river.

On a Picture of a South African Street

Our spirits grow weirder
Every night
Vengeance drags its long
And weary Shadow.

New vision could rise
From nightmare
Love and agony can light
The future.

On the farthest side of rainbow
Terror
We shall excavate the howling
Pot of human
Misery.

They Say

They say
Love grows
When the fear of death
Looms.

They say
Courage looms
When the fear
Of never loving again
Disappears
In the smell of the enemy
Who crushes us so much
We can only fight.

Love and courage grow together
When the flesh is rawest
And the spirit charged
And distorted within the nightmare
We see the possibility
Of a future.

To One Dying of Leukaemia
For F.H.

Your dream of another
Life is before you.
They have drawn the curtain
Tighter from within.
The flowers in your veins
Grow rot while
They flow with their petals
Of life
Upon your waning face.
Your dream of another
Life is before you.

Mother surrounds you
With panic.
Her desire is to share
Your deflowering Rot
Of fate.
They now play charades before you:
Of all the happy days
In memory
The wondrous journeys
To the exotic place where
The sickle falls.
They act out fantasies
For you
They bring on childhood
Friends
And surround you with
The memories
Of Old China.

And yet you know
That your dream of another
Life is before you.

They do not know
Your terror.
Their twists of love
Are like tender innocence
With fangs that
Fear death
And fear you.
They no longer share
Your hunger
For rich tapestries
And fashion fingers
Weighted with rings
Of pearl and jade
Or for the smell
Of jasmine tea
On a wintry day.

They process you
In stories
To friends.
They no longer share
The fastening
Of your eyes.
They do not see things
As you do
With the special
Sadness
Of one at the blue
Door
Departing without
A smile.
They fear your
Grey eyes
That gaze now

Into that eternity
Of silence.
Your dream of another
Life is behind you.

1984

The Incandescence of the Wind

The incandescence of the wind
bothers me
in this vineyard.
Is there a searing clarity
about the noises
rising daily .
from this riverbed we call our own?

The yam-tubers bleed our sorrows.
Crows in the fields
scream of despair.
Machetes pollute our food
with rust.
The masters conduct their
plunderings
with quiet murders:
The victims perform maypole dances
around the village shrines.

There is a cold fire in the air.
I hear it
consume the groins
of heroes
and shrivel the guts
of martyrs.
The name of the fire
is printed on grave stones:
names squeezed from tubers of life
and collective cowardice.

At night mothers scream
of children lost in the city fires
of children lost in neon signs
and cellars of madness.
I hear noises from the streets:

men are lost in files
or have wandered
into the fractured severity
of military gun-shots
have become a generation
drenched in petrol
camp-fired
and barbecued
in the fevers
of elections
riots
coups.

The incandescence in the air
burns inward.
Is there a name for this fear?
Is there a fearful country
in these fields
where such realities are
manufactured whole?

I heard a secret
in the burning iron of the mornings.
Animals
have delivered eggs of blood.
Women
have discovered the secret
of an inviolable flesh-haze.
There are multiple deaths
in the riverbeds
and junkyards
polluting our world
with an irascible sense
of failure.
Shall we join them

or shall we celebrate
the vision of empty offices
the short-sightedness of power.

Break the bread
of initiation into
revolt:
We shall celebrate with our
emaciated chests.
We shall clench and raise our fists
in the wonder of incandescence.

I hear a light
bursting up through
the bright blue roots
and the yellow skeletons.
We have breathed
our self-love in those bones.
We have breathed
incantations
at those worms
that ravage our serenity.

The graveyards heave.
The riverbeds sigh.
And I wake surprised:
  — the incandescence has become
    our own
  — the skeletons have reclaimed
    the lands
  — a new spirit breathing phosphorous
    has grown
    into the blue roots of the times.

August 1982

Darkening City: Lagos, 83

For Odia Ofeimun

Our lanterns flicker at crossroads.

The mad city coughs its pollutions
On figures in the streets.

Wastage in wild corners
Breeds anger in others.

Acids boil outside
Crooked towers of state

Where politicians disgorge our lives
In vomitoriums of power.

We rush through heated garbage days
With fear in morbid blood-raw eyes:

Mobs in cancerous slums
Burn the innocent and guilty

At noon. Angled faces in twisted
Patterns of survival,

Assaults with bitter humour
And money-madness

In squandered times proclaim —
That the living itself is squeezed.

Our lanterns flicker
In darkening city

Of murderous powers without light.

II

Naked city with music
In maelstroms:

Fires, rankling
Deaths and omens

Introduce us — the minds
Of exodus — moving deeper

Into chaos. We are the measure
Of fevers. All our dreams

Are gripped in self-seeking
Towers. Eruptions everyday

In secret and garish view
Brand us that betray action.

We shore status and security
Against the mania.

Lanterns twitch and bare
The naked city in wild seasons.

III

City of tainted mirrors!
City of chaotic desires!

We are bound
One to one to all

In drooping flames
And vicious spasms

With cloudbursts above us.
We hold future fires

We hold future clarity in ash of time
And time of music

In an assault on our
Birds of prey.

Darkening city of all our loves
Our lives

An image festers in this landscape
Of scattered passions;

Cameos of terror
Tremors everywhere –

Lanterns crushed at crossroads.

An African Elegy

We are the miracles that God made
To taste the bitter fruit of Time.
We are precious.
And one day our suffering
Will turn into the wonders of the earth.

There are things that burn me now
Which turn golden when I am happy.
Do you see the mystery of our pain?
That we bear poverty
And are able to sing and dream sweet things

And that we never curse the air when it is warm
Or the fruit when it tastes so good
Or the lights that bounce gently on the waters?
We bless things even in our pain.
We bless them in silence.

That is why our music is so sweet.
It makes the air remember.
There are secret miracles at work
That only Time will bring forth.
I too have heard the dead singing.

And they tell me that
This life is good
They tell me to live it gently
With fire, and always with hope.
There is wonder here

And there is surprise
In everything the unseen moves.
The ocean is full of songs.
The sky is not an enemy.
Destiny is our friend.

February 1990

Memories Break
For Kole Omotoso

Memories break
On the shores of desire
Against the furnace of the air
And on the fingers burnt in our fires
Of survival.

Anger breaks
In lacerations of flesh
At the garages
In the fever houses;
It poisons the bubbles of laughter
Contorts our bodies
Turns exile into insanity
And to a sickly green
The beacons
Of our illogical futures.

Dreams break
On the cables of the nerves
Snapped
By a small truth
By any old picture of our journeys
Round and round the same points
By random voices in the dark
That speak to one another
From the flatness of our recession:
 — 'did you listen to the news?'
 — 'there's a new American comedy'
 — 'the lights have returned'
 — 'the children might have a bit
  of chicken tomorrow'
 — 'the troubles in the streets
  have nothing to do with us'
We can turn to one another

See blood change to water.
Wc can read hope in the clouds.
We reach for the hope
And it dissolves in our palms.
We can also note the weather
And realise how much the air
Has darkened.

The fumes have coloured our eyes
The tar dripping from the sky
Will sharpen the edge of our coffee
And we will note with pleasure
That the times we live in
Stretch the spirit's
Resilient elasticity
Twisting dreams into lily-headed
Chimeras
Reshaping the future into things
That grow upwards
Without roots, without the earth.

Fear breaks
Into organic multiples
Of itself
We watch ourselves growing smaller
The mirror reverses the image
Fixes it
Feeds it
We celebrate our future deaths
We cut out the tongues
Of our prophets
We hail our murderers
We gild our traitorous leaders
We poison our healers

And we walk with eyes wide open
Into our own abyss.
And while the vultures fly lower
And the mechanism of fear takes a face
And plunders the night
We must declare
Anything.

Truth breaks
In illogicalities
In the merciless waves
Of our ruin
Of the booms that last only a while
Before other booms come along
And smother us
Into a people who could not say NO
When the rain fell
And each drop was a drop of fear
When the thunders laughed
And strife descended.
And children leaping over ropes
Froze for a moment
Watched their stomachs bloat
And before their collapse
Understood that history is the whisper
Of rain
The smell of rain clouds before dinner
The grumble of thunder
Within the hard shell of pillow
The hint of cataclysms
In the scratchings of rats.
Declare
Only Declare.

Break this cycle
Break this madness
Let new fevers rise in this
Radiant act of faith
Destroy this temple of living hell
Let us join our angers together
Forge a new joy for the age.
Before our lives disintegrate

Create
New breaks.

August 1982

Living is a Fire

Living is a cross
That any one of the rock-faces
Comprehends.

We are drawn
To many seas.
We drown wholesomely
In the failures of confrontation.
The rain
Drenching
Our doorsteps
Has nothing to do
With the simplest desires
And lacerations
We bring
To the smallest acts
Of living.

The child
On the broken catwalk
Hearing the sounds of our hunger
Without understanding
Throws echoes back
To the earliest abandonments
Of love.

Minor devastations preceding
Horror
Resonate the ineffable.
The mothers that wake
At the slightest sound
And the fathers that
Smoke all night
And the rest of us who are

Vigilantes from the demons
Of oppressed sleep
Find at dawn the clearest
Images of our bewilderment.
Even the best things
Collapse beneath the weight
Of ignorance.

Living is a fire
That any one of the wave-lashes
Comprehends.

On Edge of Time Future

I remember the history well:
The soldiers and politicians emerged
With briefcases and guns
And celebrations on city nights.

They scoured the mess
Reviewed our history
Saw the executions at dawn
Then sighed with secret policemen

And decided something
Had to be done.

They scoured the mess
Resurrected old blue-prints
Of vicious times
Tracked the shapes of sinking cities

And learned at last
That nothing can be avoided
And so avoided everything.
I remember the history well.

2

We emerged from our rubbish mounds
Discovered a view of the sky
As the air danced in heat.

Through the view of the city
In flames, we rewound times
Of executions at beaches.
Salt streamed down our brows.

Everywhere stagger victims of rigged elections

Monolithic accidents on hungry roads
The infinite web of ethnic politics
Power-dreams and fevered winds.

The nation was a map stitched
From the grabbing of future flesh
And became a rush through
Historical slime.

3

We emerged on edge
Of time future
With bright fumes
From burning towers.

The fumes lit political rallies.
We started a war
Ended it
And dreamed about our chance.

Fat fish eat little fish
Big ones arrange executions
And armed robberies.
Our rubbish shapes us all.

I remember the history well.
The tiger's snarl is bought
In currencies of silence.
Eggs grow large:

A monstrous face is hatched.
On the edge of time future
I am a boy
With running sores

Of remembered history
Watching the stitches widen
Waiting for the volcano's laughter
In the fevered winds

Hearing the gnash
Of those who will join us
At the mighty gateways
With new blue-prints

With dew as seal
And fire as constant
And a trail through time past
To us

Who remember the history well.
We weave words on red
And sing on the edge of blue.
And with our nerves primed

We shall spin silk from rubbish
And frame time with our resolve.

1983

Ile-Ife, 86

For Maggie McKernan

When we arrived at Ife
The afternoon's heat was insistent
Like a hangover which never leaves.
The inhabitants eyed us.
Hunger and death and the passions
Of a rigged history had altered
Their collective features.

And while we — strangers from hectic
Cities — stared with amazement
At a town that was so quiet
Under the heat mists
The inhabitants merely regarded us
With the silent fever
Of their eyes.

On arriving at Ife
There was the sadness
Of a love like a trapped butterfly
A love that could not soar
In that air of yellow dust
With dogs curled up in abandoned garages
With three-legged cats limping
In the shadows of juggernauts
And with the afternoon's heat insistent
Like a fever which never leaves.

I See Your Face

I see your face
Where beauty is threatened
With violence
Roseate in the evening's
Chimerical murders.

Your face is angled at me
Like cubist lines catching
Innocence at calvary:
You trap misery
With a smile.

I see it at the window
Contemplating unhappy bodies
In the skyline
I see it by the river
Washing away the terror
Washed in from all
The junkyards battle-grounds slum-burials
Bleeding revolution.

Your face crowds me at the mortuaries
Defying the nakedness that is prodded
Packed and re-packed into a new
Geometry dreading the old
Dreading any resemblance to the bodies
maddened in the streets
Or to the nakedness tossing serenely
On a bed heaving heat.

Your face smiles at me
When at the first rung of chaos
Soldiers carry out a dying wish
Showering bullets into bodies bound

For ever with our hunger
Smashing our essences
Understanding thunder
Jerking wildly on the red sheets
With us watching crescendos spraying
Death-wash into
Our direst wonders.

I see your face
Seeing us mashed into lying
Pounded into hopelessness
Praised into submission
Starved into inhumanity
Cracked-down into circles
Where we laugh surprised
At our empty affirmations.

I see your face
As I ask kissing the razor's edge
What can we do
In this fear-chamber of our lives?
What can we do
When the lights blink back the darkness
Which seems to stay for ever?
What can we do
When the roads open out the deaths
We will confront at another turning?
What can we do
When the eyes of authority
Spatter blood on the children?
When the cold grey of the evenings
Brings in all the smells
Bearing the deaths
Of so many

Whose lives seemed septic
Who were born saying yes and died
Trying
Trying to find an alternative?
What can we do
When we see the clouds swollen
With the blood of our futures?
What can we say
When poets lie
When politicians never
Tell the secret truths
That sell us
At the world's marketplace?
What can we say
When we know we should
Be doing something
About living our lives in brutal cycles?
The logic belongs to someone else
There is no music here
We have been dancing
On the burning logs
The razor's teeth
The meat of our days
There is no music here.

And when I see your face
See it cry
See it weep the blood we know is ours
See it twitch and grin out our deepest hours
See it transform its beauty
Shocked by the flowering of bodies
Putrescent in our lives
When I see it
I see many faces in one —

Break this sacrament
this heart this fire
Share this body back to its
original multitude
as we scream into
the fumes of the air:
There is no music here
When we are shot there is only an
Illusion of music
Which the frenzy itself transmits
This is no way to live
When we can die
Holding our bodies by the invisible levers
And fight these temples that plague
Our bones;
There are no flowers here
We squashed them on other days
As we spun the confusion of our ways
And we must come back
To where the earth is smouldering
To where the smells curl on themselves
To where the flesh is raw at every street-corner
To where the mind is seared by the smell of dawn
To where the spirit tramps the million crevices of fear
To where this old animal stalks starving
To where this old flesh breathes death
To where it is hardest to begin
    Where we must scream clarity on chaos
    Scream simple terror on complacency
    Scream blood on blood
            Water on water
            The pigs drowned yesterday
            The prophet went with them
            The sea now possesses us.

And do I see your face
Watching this new design
Lifting on each wind?
I know that
When we have been deposited
In this cauldron
Which widens in the smithy's fire
          in the electric tremors
           when the dawns have become
           too much
And widened to each point in our battlegrounds
To each
To each
To each
I know
There will be faces
With yours and mine.

                      Ife, 1982

I Shall Tell You

I shall tell you
The meaning of love
When the conflagrations
In the cities
Subside.

We will show you
The skeleton's peculiar beauty
When the buryings
Have been accomplished
When the blood
Of military music
Has groaned out
And when the babies freshly
Delivered
In the pogrom
Have survived.

When mothers learn to forget
And the rest of us turn
Our eyes expectantly
To the skyline
When the new generation
Begins to ask questions
To rage and dissent
We shall explain the mystery
Of spirit
The magic of touch
The genesis of warm breath
On face.

When the time has incinerated itself
And heroes erected from ash
And new images furnished for our sanity

Maybe we will learn to love again
As we struggle in the throes of history.

1983

And If You Should Leave Me

And if you should leave me
I would say that the ghost
Of Cassandra
Has passed through
My eyes
I would say that the stars
In their malice
Merely light up the sky
To stretch my torment
And that the waves crash
On the shores
To bring salt-stings on
My face:
For you re-connect me with
All the lights of the sky
And the salt of the waves
And the myths in the air.
And with your passing
The evening would become too dark
   To dream in
And the morning
   Too bright.

March 1986

You Walked Gently Towards Me

You walked gently towards me
In the evening light
And brought silence with you
Which fell off when
I touched your shoulder
And felt the rain on it.

We went through the city
Up the roaring streets
Full of many lights
And we sought a place
To be alone
And found none.

The evening was merciful
On your smile.
Your laughter touched
The hungry ghosts
Of passing years.

You moved smoothly
On the waters
Your shadow sounded of silk
You led me to places
Full of mellow darkness
Secret coves where they
Didn't let us in
And under the rain
You bid me kiss you with
Your silent and uncertain eyes.

We walked home
And the rain laughed around us
With its insistent benediction

And your hair was strung with
      Diadems
Your face with glittering dreams
And my eyes were wet
      With your luminous spirited joy.

                March 1986

I Held You in the Square

I held you in the square
And felt the evening
Re-order itself around
Your smile.

The dreams I could never touch
Felt like your body.
Your gentleness made the
Night soft.

And even if we didn't know
Where we were going,
Nor what street to take
Or what bench to sit on
What chambers awaited
That would deliver us our
Naked joy,
I could feel in your spirit
The restlessness for a journey
Whose beauty lies
In the arriving moment
Of each desire.

Holding you in the evening square,
I sealed a dream
With your smile as the secret pact.

March 1986

Demolition Street: London, 83

Concrete lights were with him
That year
The lights fell on mouldy walls
Danced on the devil's face.
He lived alone: around him
The tenements collapsed;
He breathed in their fumes.

The children around
Played naked games:
With faces dyed
In the deserted street
They sang no songs.

Mountainous rubble
And aluminium fences
Hid them from the corpses
Of cats;
Alleyways of garbage
Hid them from dogs
Copulating
On lonely nights
And from rats that
Invaded their listless
Quietude.

2

Rubble lights played on
Broken walls.
The faces of the undercities
Were on the windows
Patched with rags.
There were no rooms
He could explore.

The children saw the spaces
Collapse amongst them:
The dead street held
Small enchantments.
When they began to hear
The invasion of the rats
They fell silent.

Across in the air
Tower blocks gleamed
With their joyless
Murals.
He heard the children
Talk about history
In the cold afternoons:
The shadows of the tower blocks
Were over them.

3
Then faces in the street
Disappeared;
Lorries came; the children
Left; and at noon
He watched the procession
Of families
Through the rags.
How strange it felt: a cold
Day with the children
Going.
He saw their possessions:
Old collections of ruined clothes
With memories
Soaked in their grime:
Memories of new days in a new

Country
With conquests before them.

Memories sit obscenely
On weathered faces
Murky faces of children
Old before their time.
He saw their dented pots
And pans
Their clothes from another
Era:
They loaded the lorries
With good grace.
The day was kind to them.

They left and the wind
Roamed the street.
Other children scurried at morn
Down its solitude
And fled from school
To fantasies.

4

And fire came
With the nights.
Those that remained
In the street
Woke and listened
To the burnings:
The smell of burnt flesh
Ruined the breath
Of the night:
They rushed out and saw
Their houses flaming.

Fire brought flight
And dark lorries
With drivers dozing and
Nodding in dreams
Of resentment and finance.
One way or another
We yield to ourselves:
The best intentions
Yield a passageway to desire
And the awkward dreams of power.

5

And as the last families
Began moving away towards safety
He saw demolitions
Trailing them.
He stayed behind
And watched the houses
Collapse
One by one by day:
At night through windows
He saw couples streak past
Tossing on beds
Fighting afterwards:
Even sex led them away
From themselves.
The electric shadows
On crumbling walls
Made him lonely.
Rising damp graphed his
Ecstasy.

At dawn rats bared their teeth
At the shadow of lions:

It takes courage
To count the teeth.
Celebrate whichever ones
Still survive.

6

He went beyond the walls
And found the city waiting.
Blackened carpets
And battered chairs
And unread books and clothes
And mouldy dreams
Moved their humped shapes
On the backs of the new wraiths.
How silent the women were.
How the children swore beneath
The slumber of the airless street.

If they all listened
They might have heard
The drill of the undercities
The whistles and the screams
And the muffled ironclad feet
And the unsheathed fingernails gouging
Scratching clutching at dreams.
They might have heard
The feet that thud out special
Sounds of victims stalking
Themselves beneath the city walls
Breathing metal spikes
Following doors marked with
Special exits
Leading to themselves
In silent rooms

Where they always have to listen hard
And listen beneath the reassuring
Noises of radio, music, television.

They might hear their footsteps
Later on
That lead away
And lead back again
To themselves in steaming halls
With laughter and despair all about them
With songs of rage and sadness
Morality and smoke-fed consolation.

And the city waited.
He saw concrete lights
Metal spikes
Lips so hard
Wired teeth
And there was heat with the thirst
And there was water and poison
Everywhere
And later he saw the youths
In psychiatric wards
History confuses
They must believe what they must
Salvation is freedom
And they died at police stations
And were shot from behind
And were turned pulp for law and order
Like Oluwale who tramped Leeds
And two policemen baptised his body
On the river that brought slaves
And when they fished him out
Lies were necessary

Who can tell a truth like that?

7

The concrete hit him one day
With lights from demolition balls.
He fell and slept
On the city floors.
And they beat him while he slept
And he woke purified.
He found his feet
And found his eyes
And walked on rivers
Of stone
Hauling his lies with him,
Homeward bound.
He was a fool
And only learned this much:
He must find freedom from colour –
While the mindless light of concrete power
Stalks him and many.

A Gentle Requiem

Images of your face
Bring me
The wild mane of summer leaves
And the sound of creepers on windows.

Terror is you in the distance
The wind on mad waters
The smell of incense in abattoirs
Brushing sleep into unclean corners.

Gyrating dreams weave on time
Designs of chaos.
Ice throttles silence: air animates rust.
Beneath water fire-shells survive.

Then sometimes in deep weather a door bursts open:
Lights thread the shadow
Waters run riot, and the colours of death
Crystallise lions in panic.

Beneath pain fire-dreams revive.
Waves rush over glass
Leaving only a ripple
On your face.

Political Abiku

He returned again
And again
Through her parturition
With executions on his fingers
With numberless deaths
As his ring of pearls.
And full of the crop
Of silent
Massacres
Was his stomach.

       a movement seeps into
       silent pogroms
       with music on our veins.

Flesh-tubers were her funeral
Weights
Dragging life-force back
To the earth
And to our reservoir of pain.
Sweat on our cracks leaked
Laughter.

We heard her weep
In our evening's settled
Dust of betrayals.
We felt her convulsions
We awaited the startled cries
At crossroads
After rain.
We heard none:
And only stories scratched
On mirrors
Record the fall of lifeless weight.

And many die
Knowing so little.

Outside the earth-mound
Gateway to his death
We heard her scream:
'Never again, Abiku-seed,
Never to my body return.'
We prayed for the purification
Of rain.
It came
And with it, blood.
Her fever ran runnels
To our ghettos:
Children played
While corruption flowed
With the secret flood.

2

With the harmattan
She bloomed.
Her laughter crackled
The weeds
And there was festivity
In the air.

Funfairs grow
With our strife:
Celebrations tend
Our crooked history.

Lies on the face of peace
Incinerate the dawn.
Ashes tell no truths.

The fires in the square
Breathe opiates
On raw faces.
And as we dance to the
Renewing metallic dawn
And go mad on beds of fumes
We betray our limitless
Imagination
In the midst of national
Strife.
There's a time for healing
A time to retrench
And a time to declare
Secret coffins
For the state.

3

Then one morning
When salt-rain presaged
Necessity on thunder-tips
She screamed again:
The birth-pains had returned
And another bloody
Parturition wracked our
Demented nation.

Two friends were shot
Asking a question
And we stalked all the years
Moving beneath cables
Awaiting chinks of opportunities
We got drunk
Talked about our achievements
Celebrated our manufactured

Hindsight
Steamed our hollows
With noise:
And the birth-pains had long returned
Had never left.

Our chaos had become fodder
For those who manipulate
Our history
On their determinations
For their finance.
The circle widens
Where should
The cables lead?
Our fingers bless
The seepages of state.
How many burned for it?

She howled
At the air of waste
The excess bile
The money-dreams
Our worn-out complacency
And promises of action
With the decayed boom
On bitter faces.

At twisted junctions
Angled faces
Plan detonations through
The undercities.
The cables lead to the
Other screams
And to her besides the gateway

Waiting for purifying
Rain.
How many move for it?

1983

We Have No Other Way

We have no other way
Through the blistering
Air of our lives.
The miasma is ours.

The night denies our participation
Sunlight breaks on our anguish.
How many smothered faces
Does it take to establish
Our disquiet?
How many fractured limbs
Will it take
To rebuild in the quietude
Of waiting?

A domain descends
And scalds ash from
Our brains.
We stalk on the crater's precipice
Arguing subtleties
Beneath the brows
Of pitiless gods.

2

We have no other way
But to chart
Beneath the skin's anointed pain
And above the flames
Of the head.

We have no choice but to live
More intensely
While the armies gather
And the earth widens for our fears.

3

May the wisdom of roots prevail
That we may see the eyes
Of monsters bloat at our terror.
They might blast their strange detonators
But we shall reply
With salted love in our wounds
With geometry
And religion in our violence.
We shall breach the walls
       breathe cracks on the mirrors
       and dare the white cock
       with its feathers.
We shall be there
When our lives begin.

4

Our limbs imitate flight.
We shall metamorphose our loss
Widen the angles
And increase the height
And depth
Of the body's tameless spirit.

Plagues that growl our secret names
Leave us staggering
With inhuman love.
Transformations that occur
Within the mind's heaving
Recess
Bequeath us
The shores of human desires
And the dreams of a compassionate god.

5

The lights of secret volcanoes call us

Blending fires and water temper us
The night dares us
Sunlight charges us:
         We must breath anew
         And anoint the spirit
                  in coolest
                  burning
                  dew.

                  1983

The Poet Declares

It comes for us all at different times.
It comes for us all
   this wind of metallic shivers
   this icy hand of November
   in a strange season
When boldness flees the mind
And the sharpness of an
                        inexorable white fate
                        breaks upon the towering dream
                        of ranging the world
And journeying with the stars
                        whose fire is but
                        an illumination of the soul.

It comes upon us all at different times
   this quaking of our spirit's foundation
   this bursting of the devil's banks
   this explosion of primordial powers
   this mindful infiltration by our heavenly fears.

From red eyes and burnt fingers
                        in this rusted month of ice
I connect the embers of an
                        ancient dream —
Let the music irradiate my spirit
      And I shall travel farther than allowed
      to find the gifts of the new
                        light.

1986

Restore the Balance

For Davina Doughan

Dance of the triumphant
Silence

Serenity and Grace
Conquer
The chaos gently

And love always with mood
And music
Restores the balance
Which time transforms
Into forgotten moments –

Paris, March 1991

And Anyone Who Doesn't

And anyone who doesn't
Tremble
At the gates
Of reality
Will be broken
By what they encounter
In the city
And its secret dungeons
And its history which
Keeps rising.

At the gate of each
Unnameable
Reality
It is possible
To lose
A fear
And an illusion:
It is possible
To witness
Miracles
In your life –
By surprising
Your destiny.

July 1985

To an English Friend in Africa

For Daisy Waugh

Be grateful for the freedom
To see other dreams.
Bless your loneliness as much as you drank
Of your former companionships.
All that you are experiencing now
Will become moods of future joys
So bless it all.
Do not think your way superior
To another's
Do not venture to judge
But see things with fresh and open eyes
Do not condemn
But praise when you can
And when you can't, be silent.

Time now is a gift for you
A gift of freedom
To think and remember and understand
The ever perplexing past
And to re-create yourself anew
In order to transform time.

Live while you are alive.
Learn the ways of silence and wisdom
Learn to act, learn a new speech
Learn to be what you are in the seed of your spirit
Learn to free yourself from all the things
That have moulded you
And which limit your secret and undiscovered road.

Remember that all things which happen
To you are raw materials
Endlessly fertile

Endlessly yielding of thoughts that could change
Your life and go on doing so forever.

Never forget to pray and be thankful
For all things good or bad on the rich road;
For everything is changeable
So long as you live while you are alive.

Fear not, but be full of light and love;
Fear not, but be alert and receptive;
Fear not, but act decisively when you should;
Fear not, but know when to stop;
Fear not, for you are loved by me;
Fear not, for death is not the real terror,
But life – magically – is.

Be joyful in your silence
Be strong in your patience
Do not try to wrestle with the universe
But be sometimes like water or air
Sometimes like fire
And constant like the earth.

Live slowly, think slowly, for time is a mystery.
Never forget that love
Requires always that you be
The greatest person you are capable of being,
Self-regenerating and strong and gentle –
Your own hero and star.

Love demands the best in us
To always and in time overcome the worst
And lowest in our souls.
Love the world wisely.

It is love alone that is the greatest weapon
And the deepest and hardest secret.

So fear not, my friend.
The darkness is gentler than you think.
Be grateful for the manifold
Dreams of creation
And the many ways of the unnumbered peoples.

Be grateful for life as you live it.
And may a wonderful light
Always guide you on the unfolding road.

March 1991